nickelodeon The PENGUINS of MADAGASCAR™

DreamWorks®

PENGUINS ON A MISSION

COMIC READER
by Arie Kaplan

GROSSET & DUNLAP
An Imprint of Penguin Group (USA) Inc.

GROSSET & DUNLAP
Published by the Penguin Group
Penguin Group (USA) Inc., 375 Hudson Street, New York, New York 10014, USA
Penguin Group (Canada), 90 Eglinton Avenue East, Suite 700, Toronto,
Ontario M4P 2Y3, Canada (a division of Pearson Penguin Canada Inc.)
Penguin Books Ltd., 80 Strand, London WC2R 0RL, England
Penguin Group Ireland, 25 St. Stephen's Green, Dublin 2, Ireland
(a division of Penguin Books Ltd.)
Penguin Group (Australia), 250 Camberwell Road, Camberwell, Victoria 3124,
Australia (a division of Pearson Australia Group Pty. Ltd.)
Penguin Books India Pvt. Ltd., 11 Community Centre,
Panchsheel Park, New Delhi—110 017, India
Penguin Group (NZ), 67 Apollo Drive, Rosedale, North Shore 0632, New Zealand
(a division of Pearson New Zealand Ltd.)
Penguin Books (South Africa) (Pty.) Ltd., 24 Sturdee Avenue,
Rosebank, Johannesburg 2196, South Africa

Penguin Books Ltd., Registered Offices: 80 Strand, London WC2R 0RL, England

ISBN 978-0-448-45410-8   10 9 8 7 6 5 4 3 2 1

THE PENGUINS

SKIPPER
COMMANDER OF THE PENGUIN POSSE. A NATURAL-BORN LEADER.

KOWALSKI
BRAINIAC OF THE GROUP.

RICO
DEMOLITIONS EXPERT. HAS ALL SORTS OF THINGS IN HIS STOMACH (SKATEBOARD, ETC.) AND CAN "RETRIEVE" THEM AT ANY TIME.

PRIVATE
WIDE-EYED AND NAIVE, PRIVATE IS READY FOR ANYTHING.

THE LEMURS

KING JULIEN
SELF-PROCLAIMED RULER OF THE ZOO—AND PARTY ANIMAL.

MAURICE
KING JULIEN'S SENSIBLE RIGHT-HAND LEMUR.

MORT
KING JULIEN'S BIGGEST FAN.

FRIENDS

MARLENE
PLAYFUL OTTER WHO LOVES TO RELAX AND HAVE FUN WITH THE PENGUINS OR THE LEMURS.

FOES

ALICE
BEFUDDLED ZOOKEEPER WHO'S ALWAYS ONE STEP BEHIND THE PENGUINS' ANTICS.

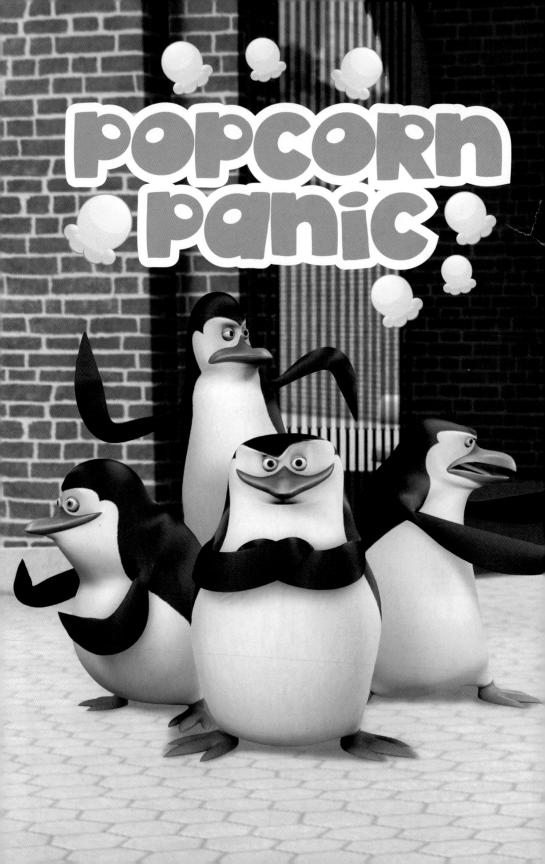

THE PENGUINS WANTED POPCORN—BAD.
SO SKIPPER PUT "OPERATION POPCORN"
INTO FULL EFFECT.

LOOK ALIVE, MEN.
TIME TO GET US
SOME POPCORN.

SKIPPER AND PRIVATE DISTRACTED AN
UNSUSPECTING POPCORN EATER . . .

. . . WHILE KOWALSKI PUNCTURED A
HOLE IN HIS POPCORN CONTAINER.

GULP!
GULP!
GULP!

HUH?

5

THE PENGUINS WERE PLEASED WITH ALL THE POPCORN THEY HAD RECEIVED.

OUTSTANDING!

THE OTHER ANIMALS WERE COLLECTING POPCORN, TOO.

DANCE, MORT! DANCE FOR THE SILLY HUMANS AND THEY THROW THE DELICIOUS POPPITY CORN AT US!

POPCORN, I LIKE THIS!

THE CHILDREN THREW POPCORN AT JULIEN AND MORT.

AND MARLENE CHARMED THE HUMANS INTO GIVING HER POPCORN.

EVERYTHING WAS GOING WELL UNTIL . . .

DID YOU KNOW THAT EVERY LAST BEASTIE IN THIS ZOO IS ON A VERY SPECIAL DIET?

. . .ALICE THE ZOOKEEPER STEPPED IN.

SHE WASN'T GOING TO LET THEM EAT ANY MORE POPCORN! SOMETHING HAD TO BE DONE.

THE ANIMALS HELD AN EMERGENCY MEETING AT THE ZOOVENIR SHOP.

ALICE HAS CLAMPED DOWN. SHE'S ACTUALLY ENFORCING THE "DO NOT FEED THE ANIMALS" POLICY.

I CAN'T LIVE WITHOUT POPCORN!

POPCORN!

POPCORN!

POPCORN!

WE MUST GET RID OF THAT INSANE ZOOKEEPER ALICE.

NEGATORY. YOU'LL JUST GET MORE ALICES IN HER PLACE.

NO ONE COULD DECIDE WHO SHOULD BE IN CHARGE OF SOLVING THE NO-POPCORN PROBLEM.

HOW COULD I NOT BE IN CHARGE?

FAILURE IS NOT AN OPTION.

I VOTE FOR YOU!

LET'S GET A LITTLE CREATIVE HERE. WHAT IF WE WORK TOGETHER TO GET THE POPCORN?

THE PENGUINS HATCHED THEIR PLAN. THAT NIGHT, THEY BROKE INTO THE SNACK STORAGE FACILITY.

THE PENGUINS GRABBED A BAG OF POPCORN. BUT THE LEMURS NABBED IT FROM THEM!

FINDERS KEEPERS!

ENGUINS GRABBED BAG. THEN, EVERYONE TED TO CHOW DOWN.

PREPARE TO EAT POPCORN UNTIL YOUR GUTS EXPLODE!

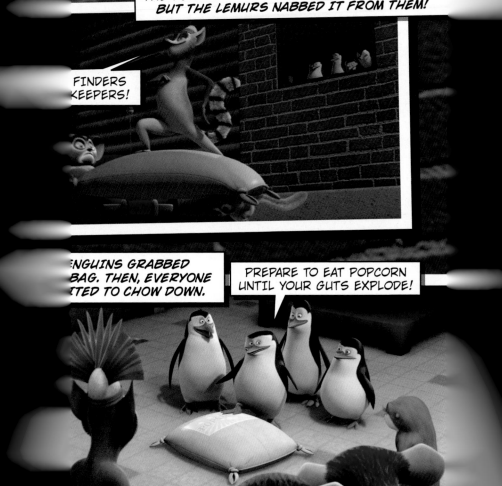

BUT WHEN THEY SAW THE UNPOPPED KERNELS, THEY WERE PUZZLED.

THIS DOESN'T LOOK ANYTHING LIKE THE PICTURE ON THE BAG.

UH-OH! ALICE WAS COMING! EVERYONE FROZE. SHE SHONE HER FLASHLIGHT AROUND THE ROOM BUT DIDN'T SEE THEM.

LATER, THE LEMURS SAT ON THE KERNELS, THINKING THEY WERE POPCORN EGGS THAT NEEDED TO BE HATCHED.

I THINK MINE'S HATCHING!

MEANWHILE, PRIVATE NOTICED A PROBLEM.

SKIPPER! OUR BAG SPRUNG A LEAK.

A QUICK LOOK THROUGH THE PERISCOPE REVEALED THAT SOMEONE ELSE NOTICED THE LEAK, TOO.

I THINK ALICE MIGHT BE ONTO US!

THE PENGUINS SCRAMBLED TO HIDE THE KERNELS.

THE INCINERATOR'S THE LAST PLACE SHE'LL EVER LOOK.

WITH THE KERNELS IN THE FURNACE, ALICE DIDN'T SUSPECT A THING.

IT'S LIKE NOTHING HAPPENED.

BUT SOON, EVERYONE FELT A RUMBLING. MORT THOUGHT IT WAS HIS POPCORN EGG.

IT'S HATCHING!

THE FURNACE POPPED THE POPCORN KERNELS ALL AT ONCE, CAUSING AN EXPLOSION OF POPCORN!

IT'S A POP-STORM! OR IS IT A CORN-ADO?

AND ALICE WAS HELPLESS TO DO ANYTHING ABOUT IT.

OF COURSE, JULIEN THOUGHT THAT THIS TSUNAMI OF TASTY TREATS WAS ALL HIS DOING.

THE SALTY SNACK GODS HAVE CHOSEN TO REWARD ME!

AFTER THE PENGUINS HAD ENJOYED THEIR FAIR SHARE OF THE SALTY SNACK, THEY WERE EXHAUSTED.

YOU KNOW, MEN, I'M ACTUALLY PRETTY DARN SICK OF POPCORN.

THE END!

TANGLED IN THE WEB

SKIPPER WAS NERVOUS. HE WAS SURE THE PENGUINS WERE BEING WATCHED, BUT HE COULDN'T FIGURE OUT WHY.

EVER FEEL LIKE SOMEONE'S WATCHING YOUR EVERY MOVE?

SO HE LED THE PENGUINS ON A MISSION TO FIND OUT.

FOLLOW MY LEAD.

KOWALSKI, RE-CON!

KOWALSKI WHIPPED OUT HIS BINOCULARS . . .

. . . AND SAW A WEIRD CAMERA STARING AT HIM.

THERE WERE CAMERAS EVERYWHERE!
THE PENGUINS TRIED TO HIDE.

THEY ZIGZAGGED ALL OVER THE HABITAT, TRYING
TO GET AWAY FROM THE CAMERAS. IT WAS NO USE.

STILL THERE.
STILL WATCHING.

ALICE WAS INSTALLING MORE CAMERAS AS SHE TALKED INTO HER WALKIE-TALKIE.

I STILL THINK THIS WHOLE INTERNET THING IS STUPID. WHO WANTS TO WATCH ANIMALS ON A COMPUTER?

LATER THAT NIGHT, MARLENE EXPLAINED TO THE ANIMALS THAT THESE WERE WEBCAMS. PEOPLE COULD WATCH THE ANIMALS ON THEIR COMPUTERS.

THEN THEY VOTE FOR THEIR FAVORITE.

SKIPPER WAS SUSPICIOUS OF THE WEBCAMS.

NO, THEY'RE NOT. IT'S JUST FOR FUN.

DON'T YOU GET IT? THEY'RE TRYING TO GET INSIDE OUR HEADS.

MARLENE SHOWED JULIEN THE TROPHIES SHE WON WHEN SHE WAS AN INTERNET POPULARITY CONTEST WINNER. HE WANTED ONE FOR HIMSELF!

BUT SKIPPER DIDN'T WANT THE WEBCAMS TRACKING HIS EVERY MOVE.

HERE'S THE PLAN: WE GIVE THEM ZIP. DON'T MOVE A MUSCLE.

JULIEN WAS BUSY TRYING TO GET THE WEBCAMS TO PAY ATTENTION TO HIM.

OVER HERE!

THEY EVEN SLEPT
STANDING STILL.

THE NEXT DAY, ALICE DUMPED
A NEW BATCH OF FISH IN THE
PENGUIN'S FOOD DISH.

SKIPPER TOLD PRIVATE TO STAY STILL. BUT THEN
THE DELICIOUS FISH SMELL WAFTED PAST.

HE MADE A MAD DASH FOR THE FISH, ACCIDENTALLY STEPPING ON RICO'S ROLLER SKATE. HE ROLLED OUT OF CONTROL, SLIPPING AND FALLING ALL OVER THE PLACE.

FOLKS EVERYWHERE LOVED WATCHING THE CUTE PENGUIN SLIP AND FALL!

THEY THOUGHT HE WAS HILARIOUS!

PEOPLE CLICKED ON PRIVATE AS THEIR FAVORITE ANIMAL AGAIN AND AGAIN.

CLICK ON YOUR FAVORITE!

THE VERY NEXT MORNING, ALL THE PENGUINS WERE BACK TO STAYING STRONG.

BUT WHEN THEY WOKE UP, THEY REALIZED THERE WAS A CROWD GATHERED AROUND THEM.

HEY, SLIPPY!

SLIPPY!

THE CROWD HAD GATHERED TO SEE SOMEONE CALLED "SLIPPY."

WHO'S SLIPPY?

APPARENTLY, YOU ARE SLIPPY.

I DON'T WANT TO BE SLIPPY.

PRIVATE WAS SO POPULAR THAT JULIEN BECAME JEALOUS.

I HAVE TO HAVE THE PRETTY SHINY TROPHY, AND THE ROLY-POLY PENGUIN IS HOGGING ALL THE GLORY THAT SHOULD BE THE KING'S!

I NEED YOUR HELP! PLEASE!

MARLENE TOLD JULIEN THAT SHE HAD AN IDEA FOR A PERFORMANCE THAT WOULD KNOCK THEM DEAD.

YES, BECAUSE IF THEY ARE DEAD, THEY CANNOT VOTE FOR THAT RIDICULOUS PENGUIN.

AND JUST AS SKIPPER AND KOWALSKI WERE TRYING TO THINK OF WAYS TO OUTWIT THE WEBCAMS . . .

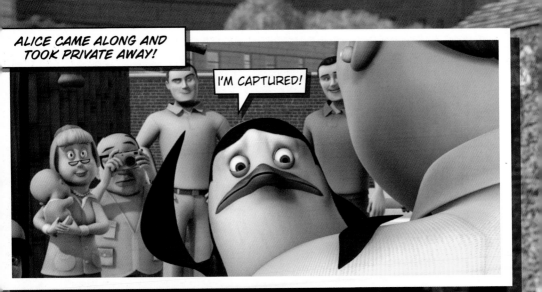

ALICE CAME ALONG AND TOOK PRIVATE AWAY!

I'M CAPTURED!

SKIPPER WAS DISTRESSED.

HE'S JUST A BOY!

ALICE PUT HIM IN HIS OWN SEPARATE HABITAT.

SLIPPY: THE WORLD'S MOST FAMOUS PENGUIN. 744,022 HITS AND COUNTING.

IT WAS SURROUNDED BY A FANTASTIC SKATE PARK!

SLIP-PY! SLIP-PY! SLIP-PY! SLIP-PY! SLIP-PY! SLIP-PY! SLIP-PY!

PRIVATE DIDN'T KNOW WHAT TO DO. BUT THEN, HE TRIPPED ONTO A ROLLER SKATE, ZOOMING UP AND DOWN THE RAMPS OF THE SKATE PARK.

THE CROWD WENT WILD!

PRIVATE WAS REWARDED WITH A HEAPING HELPING OF DELICIOUS FISH.

SLIPPY COULD GET USED TO THIS.

THAT NIGHT, SKIPPER, KOWALSKI, AND RICO WERE DETERMINED TO FREE THEIR FRIEND.

AT THE SAME TIME, JULIEN AND MARLENE WERE TRYING TO DISTRACT THE WEBCAMS WITH THEIR OWN ANTICS.

WELCOME TO CIRQUE DE SO-GREAT!

TO PERFORM HIS JAUNTY GYMNASTICS, JULIEN WAS TIED TO A ROPE, WHICH HELD HIM IN MIDAIR.

BUT MAURICE WAS HOLDING ON TO THE OTHER END OF THAT ROPE.

AND WHEN MAURICE LOST HIS GRIP, JULIEN PLUMMETED TO THE GROUND LIKE A LEAD WEIGHT!

I'M PRETTY SURE THIS AIN'T IN MY JOB DESCRIPTION.

JULIEN LANDED ON THE SEESAW MORT WAS RESTING ON, CAUSING MORT TO CATAPULT INTO THE SKY.

UH-OH.

AND AT THAT VERY MOMENT, IN PRIVATE'S "SLIPPY" HABITAT, SKIPPER AND THE OTHER PENGUINS ARRIVED.

WE'RE BUSTING YOU OUT.

OOOH, REALLY? TODAY MIGHT NOT WORK FOR ME.

JUST AS I FEARED. YOU'VE BEEN BRAINWASHED.

JUST THEN, MORT SMASHED INTO SLIPPY'S HABITAT . . .

AAAAAAHHH HA!

 ...AND GRABBED ONTO THE WEBCAM TO STOP HIMSELF.

OW.

 THE WEBCAM FLEW OFF ITS POLE AND INTO AN OPEN WINDOW, WHERE ALICE WAS SINGING AND DANCING.

PEOPLE EVERYWHERE SAW ALICE SINGING AND SHAKING HER GROOVE THING.

🎵 ON THE JUNGLE SCENE, HE IS THE FUNK 🎵 MACHINE!

THEY CLICKED ON HER AS THEIR FAVORITE AGAIN AND AGAIN.

THE NEXT DAY, SLIPPY WAS NO LONGER THE ZOO'S MOST POPULAR INTERNET ATTRACTION.

IT'S GOOD TO HAVE YOU BACK, PRIVATE.

BUT ALICE WAS.

♪ ON THE JUNGLE SCENE, HE IS THE FUNK MACHINE! ♪

I AM NOT BELIEVING THAT THE PEOPLE VOTED THIS MOST POPULAR!

THE END!

CROWN
FOOLS
THE PENGUINS WERE PRACTICING THEIR BEST BATTLE MOVES.
ALL RIGHT, MEN. WE'RE UP AGAINST NINE NINJA WARRIORS.
HIIII-YAH!

WITH A SUPER-SERIOUS LOOK ON HIS FACE, SKIPPER ASKED THE PENGUINS IF THEY THOUGHT HE WAS FUN.

UH . . . BIG FUN!

ER . . . UH, SURE!

BUT MARLENE POINTED TO THE MOST FUN GUY IN THE ZOO . . . KING JULIEN!

HA-HA-HA!

SKIPPER STARTED JUMPING ON JULIEN'S BOUNCY. JULIEN WANTED TO KNOW WHAT HE WAS DOING.

IT'S FUNDAY, AND CERTAIN SEA MAMMALS THINK I'M NO FUN.

TO PROVE HOW FUN HE WAS, SKIPPER TRIED OUT A DARING MOVE CALLED THE CORKSCREW!

BUT HE LANDED BEAK FIRST ON JULIEN'S BOUNCY, PUNCTURING IT!

MMPH!

NOOO!

AIR SHOT OUT OF THE BOUNCY, BLASTING THE CROWN OFF JULIEN'S HEAD.

THE CROWN FELL DOWN A SEWER GRATING.

AHHHHHHHHHH . . .

AHHHHHHHHH . . .

JULIEN WOULDN'T STOP YELLING ABOUT IT.

MAURICE WAS ANGRY THAT SKIPPER MADE HIS BOSS UPSET.

YOU! YOU DID THIS!

SO MARLENE CAME UP WITH A PLAN.

ALL RIGHT, I'LL TRY TO CALM DOWN THE SCREAMER WHILE YOU GUYS GO GET HIS CROWN.

AS NIGHT SET IN, MARLENE SET TO WORK COMING UP WITH A REPLACEMENT CROWN FOR JULIEN. FIRST, SHE MADE A BALLOON CROWN.

IT IS PUFFY AND COMPLICATED.

LIKE ME?

BUT THE BALLOON CROWN POPPED.

POP!

I WANT MY OLD CROWN!

MEANWHILE, THE PENGUINS WENT INTO THE SEWERS TO FIND JULIEN'S CROWN.

I DON'T LIKE THE LOOKS OF THIS.

SLAM!

WITH THAT, A CAGE SLAMMED DOWN ON THE PENGUINS.

SKIPPER, WE'RE IN THIS TOGETHER.

THIS APPEARS TO BE A FORMER LAB RAT. THUS THE EXTREME MUTATIONS.

WELL, INCREDIBLE SIZE AND BRUTE STRENGTH AND MAGNIFICENT AIM AREN'T . . . UH . . EVERYTHING . . .

T BECAME CLEAR THAT SKIPPER WAS NO MATCH FOR KING RAT'S BRUTE STRENGTH.

THAT THE BEST YOU GOT? BIRD, THAT IS SOME WEAK SAUCE!

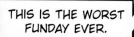

THIS IS THE WORST FUNDAY EVER.

THAT GAVE SKIPPER AN IDEA.

FUNDAY!
OF COURSE!

SKIPPER WENT INTO
HIS CORKSCREW MOVE.

HE KNOCKED THE KING
RAT TO THE MAT!

WHO'S GOT THE
WEAK SAUCE NOW?

AT THE LEMUR HABITAT, MARLENE WAS STILL TRYING TO INTEREST JULIEN IN A REPLACEMENT CROWN.

COME ON! YOU CAN BE KING OF THE COWBOYS!

WHEN ALL SEEMED LOST, THE PENGUINS SHOWED UP WITH JULIEN'S CROWN.

THE MAGIC WORD IS . . . FUNDAY!

JULIEN SEEMED HAPPY AT FIRST,
BUT HE NOTICED SOMETHING.

EH. IT HAS A
SMUDGY SPOT
ON IT.

MAURICE, BRING ME
MY SPARE CROWN.

MAURICE BROUGHT JULIEN HIS SPARE
CROWN, WHICH LOOKED EXACTLY THE
SAME AS THE FIRST CROWN.

YOU HAD A SPARE CROWN ALL ALONG??

AND MARLENE CHASED JULIEN ALL OVER THE ZOO. BUT THIS TIME, HE WAS SURE TO HOLD ON TO HIS CROWN.

THE END!